The Scrovegni Chapel in Padua

Anna Maria Spiazzi

The Scrovegni Chapel in Padua

Electa

Note

Introduction
In the first part of the guide the reader will find a brief biography of Giotto, together with a note on his works and on the success that the great artist from Mugello achieved among his contemporaries and in posterity. This is followed by an account of the events connected with the construction of the Scrovegni Chapel and with the conception of the cycle of paintings that decorates it.

The Visit
The manner in which the cycle has been reproduced permits what is in effect an illustrated book, created for the education, as well as the edification, of the faithful, to be read in the correct logical —and theological— sequence.

Appendix
The descriptions of the frescoes, sculptures and decoration of the apse and of the ornaments of the sacristy are followed by a note on the restorations to which the Chapel has been subjected over the course of the 19th and 20th centuries. Finally, an exhaustive bibliography will provide the reader with all the information needed for further investigation of the history, criticism, and significance of the cycle.

Translation
Huw Evans

Filmsetting of the text
and reproduction
of the illustrations
by Bassoli Olivieri Prestampa, Milan

Printed in Italy
© 1993 by **Electa**, Milan
Elemond Editori Associati

Contents

Historical Introduction

Giotto: His Life, Works, and Appeal

Giotto di Bondone was born at Colle di Vespignano, near Viccio di Mugello, at a date presumed to have been somewhere around 1267, given that the Florentine chronicler Antonio Pucci (c. 1348-1388) recorded his death at the age of seventy in 1337. The first major cycle of pictures that can be attributed to him—although there is no documentation for this—is the decoration of the Upper Church in Assisi with frescoes depicting *Episodes from the Life of Saint Francis*. The frescoes—commissioned, according to Vasari, by Giovanni da Murro, who was elected general of the Order of Franciscan Friars Minor in 1296, or, in the view of some critics, by Pope Nicholas IV between 1288 and 1292—are the first explicit expression of Giotto's new pictorial language and the fundamental premise for the subsequent evolution of his painting in Padua.

With the help of a collaborator who would also be active in Padua, he went on to fresco the chapel of San Nicola in the Lower Church. In the Jubilee Year he was in Rome where, according to Vasari, he frescoed the Loggia delle Benedizioni in the Lateran Palaces. Echoes of this stay in Rome can be found in the painter's adoption of a "classical" style in Padua that is absent from his earlier works, and in his renewed interest in the architecture of Arnolfo di Cambio and the sculpture of Andrea and Giovanni Pisano.

According to the testimony of Riccobaldo Ferrarese, Giotto worked for the Franciscan Order in Assisi, Rimini, and Padua. Riccobaldo's *Cronaca* (1312) tells us that, after Assisi, Giotto went to Rimini, where all that now remains is the *Cross* in the church of the Malatesta family, and to Padua. Giotto was active in Padua during the first decade of the Trecento, presumably between 1303 and 1305 and undoubtedly prior to 1309, the year in which he is recorded to have been in Assisi again. In Padua's basilica and monastery of Sant'Antonio, Giotto probably worked with his studio; the frescoes in the Chapter-house and the chapel of Santa Caterina have only survived in part and are in very poor condition. He was commissioned by Enrico Scrovegni to fresco the entire vault and walls of the chapel "of the arena": this is the best-preserved of his works, the one where his assistants contributed the least, and the most celebrated for the perfect balance between the value of its contents and of its style and form.

On his return to Assisi he decorated, with the help of his closest collaborators, the chapel of the Maddalena. The documents show him to have returned to Florence in 1312, where he undertook many works, such as the *Maestà* in Ognissanti, the *Cross* in San Felice, and the frescoes in the Peruzzi chapel. By the end of the second decade of the century, he had completed the polyptych commissioned by Cardinal Stefaneschi for the high altar of St. Peter's in Rome, and, again with the collaboration of his studio, the frescoes in the right-hand transept and vaulting cells of the Lower Church in Assisi.

We are informed by Vasari that during a second stay in Padua, presumably in 1316, he painted, or at least designed, the frescoes in the Palazzo della Ragione, on the basis of an ico-

Enrico Scrovegni (in the center between Saint John and Saint Catherine) Presenting a Model of the Chapel to the Virgin. Scrovegni Chapel, Detail of the Last Judgment.

*The Upper Basilica of San
Francesco, Assisi, View
of the interior facing the altar.*

*Saint Francis Appearing at the
Arles Chapter. Assisi, Upper
Basilica of San Francesco.*

nographic program drawn up by Pietro d'Abano. The frescoes were destroyed in the fire of 1420, but in the astrological cycle that was painted after the reconstruction of the great wooden roof, "Stefano" and Niccolò Miretto reproduced, at least in part, some of the ideas on which the decorations from the previous century were based. In Florence Giotto frescoed four chapels in Santa Croce, including the Bardi chapel. At the end of the fourth decade, he painted a large polyptych for the church of Santa Maria degli Angeli in Bologna.

There are records of his presence in Naples from 1328 to 1333, at the court of King Robert of Anjou, who described him as a member of his family: "protho pictori familiari et fideli nostro." He returned to Florence in 1334, where he was appointed master builder in charge of the work on Santa Reparata and chief engineer of the Commune. In this guise he was sent to the Visconti in Milan. Afterward he went back to Florence, where he died on 8 January 1337.

Many accounts of the artistic personality of Giotto are to be found in the writers and scholars of his own day. The first mention of him dates back to Dante: "Once, Cimabue thought to hold the field / In painting, Giotto's all the rage today; / The other's fame lies in the dust concealed" (*Purgatorio*, XI, vv. 94-96, trans. by Dorothy Sayers, Penguin Books, 1955). In the fifth tale of the sixth day of the *Decameron*, Boccaccio celebrated, through the words of the famous jurist Forese da Rabatta, Giotto's ability to depict things so much like the way they are in nature that they appear real. The great storyteller used a scheme of judgment drawn from Pliny, yet it is significant that he applied it to Giotto. Still more acute was the judgment of Petrarch who, when giving a *Madonna* by Giotto to Francesco da Carrara, the lord of Padua, underlined its beauty, which "is not understood by the ignorant, but astonishes the masters of the art." Cennino Cennini, who wrote his treatise on painting in Padua toward the end of the 14th century, described the artist's work as follows: "He transformed the art of painting from Greek to Latin, and made it modern: and his skill was the most complete that anyone ever had." He was held in no less esteem in the centuries that followed: his works were admired by Masaccio, Leonardo, Michelangelo, and Vasari. Owing to changes in taste, the historical and artistic significance of his pictorial language was ignored in the 17th century; but in the 18th, with the resumption of historical studies, his reputation was restored. In the 19th century studies by Cavalcaselle and Thode revealed the fundamental traits of the great painter's historical and artistic personality. The 20th century has seen a multitude of monographic studies and other contributions. The exhibition of Giotto's works staged in Florence in 1937 and the bibliographical corpus of studies relating to the artist are still of fundamental value today, just as are the monographic studies—to cite only some of the most important—of Toesca, Salvini, Gnudi, Previtali, and Bellosi. Rintelen, Oeffner, and Miess, like other supporters of the so-called "purist" thesis, do not accept Giotto's authorship of the frescoes in Assisi, or of any other work not strictly comparable to the frescoes in the Scrovegni chapel. And yet, for historical and stylistic reasons, it is precisely the Assisi frescoes that mark the break with the medieval era and that establish the premises for the new achievements of Giotto in the frescoes of the Scrovegni Chapel.

On the following pages: View of the Chapel looking towards the Altar (on the left) and towards the facing wall (on the right).

The Scrovegni Chapel
The documents brought to light by Tolomei (1880) provide a record of the period of the chapel's construction and of the way in which the events unfolded. On 6 January 1300 Enrico Scrovegni acquired from Delesmanini the piece of land known as the "arena" on which to build his house and chapel: "Enrico filio q. domini raynaldi scrovegni de Padova" acquired from Manfredi "filius q. domini Guezili de Delesmaninis ... arenam muris circumdatam ab omnibus lateribus excepto a latere fratruum heremitanorum de Padua cum una domo intus magna murata et solarata coperta cupis cum stupa prope posita in medio ipsius Arene cum loza post ipsam domum, et una alio domo de muro."
On 29 April 1302 Bishop Ottobono de' Razzi, who had been appointed Patriarch of Aquileia, authorized the construction of the chapel and its first consecration, recorded by a memorial tablet that has now been lost but which was transcribed by Scardeone (1560), took place on the Feast of the Annunciation, 25 March 1303: "Cum locus iste Deo solemni more dicatur / Annorum Domini tempus tunc tale notatur: / Annis mille tribus tercentum Martius almae / Virginis in festo coniuxerat ordine palmae." The inscription, as interpreted by Supino

Detail of the Last Judgment depicting the Apostles to the left of the Savior.

(1920), states that the chapel was dedicated to the Virgin in the year in which the Feast of the Annunciation came before that of Palm Sunday. In 1303, in fact, the feast days occurred on the following dates: the Annunciation on 25 March, Palm Sunday on 31 March, Easter on 7 April.

On 1 March 1304 Pope Benedict XI granted indulgence to "visitors to the church of the Blessed Virgin Mary of the Charity of the Arena in the city of Padua." On 9 January 1305 the Chapter of Augustinian Friars delivered a protest to the Bishop of Padua, claiming that Enrico Scrovegni had built a campanile with bells and a large church, with great expenditure on decoration in contravention of the instructions given to him in the concession of 1302: "nec debebat ibi aedificare magnam ecclesiam, et alia multa quae ibi facta sunt potius ad pompam et ad vanam gloriam et quaestum quam ad Dei laudem, gloriam et honorem."

On 16 March the High Council of Venice decided to allow Enrico Scrovegni to use some of the vestments from the treasury of the basilica of St. Mark for the solemn inauguration of 25 March: "cum ser Enrico Scrovegno intendat facere consecrari quandam suam capellam Paduae, et requisierit quod commodetur sibi de pannis Sanctus Marci, capta fuit pars quod possint commodari de dictis pannis." It was during the consecration that the crosses were painted on the frame of the lower row of frescoes, many of which are still visible. It can be assumed that on the day of the consecration, 25 March 1305, Giotto's frescoes were finished, since in 1306 Gerardino, per-

On the facing page, Detail of the Flight into Egypt.

The Wedding Feast in Cana, detail.

*Portraits of Saints
on the decorated bands.*

haps a painter from Bologna, was paid for a number of miniatures in the antiphonals of Padua cathedral.

The architecture of the chapel is very simple: a rectangular hall with a barrel vault, an elegant Gothic three-mullioned window on the facade, tall and narrow windows in the south wall alone, and a polygonal apse to which a belfry was added at a later date. The area of the apse does not have the transept that can be seen in the painting on the end wall representing Enrico Scrovegni dedicating the chapel to the Virgin. Neither the reasons for nor the precise date of this change are known; it can only be supposed that the modification to the original design was made during the course of the chapel's construction, since on the triumphal arch, in the area below the height of the planned transept, Giotto painted two perspective views: by representing the two cross vaults of the transept that was never built, he made use of architectural illusionism to recreate the sense of unity that the interior would have conveyed in the original design. Passing through the presbytery one comes to the sacristy, also built in the 14th century and located to the northeast. During the 16th century a loggia was built on top of the sacristy. This linked the nearby house to the chapel and had windows opening onto the apse, providing a view of liturgical ceremonies taking place in the chapel. It has been supposed that Giotto was also involved in the design of the building, but there are divergent opinions over this possibility. What is certain, however, is that before Giotto executed his decoration a door was closed on the south side, adjacent to the facade, and another opened on the north side to connect the chapel with Palazzo Scrovegni. A portico was built on the facade in the 15th century but collapsed in 1817. Nothing remains of the Scrovegni family home, reconstructed on many occasions and finally demolished in 1827.

When Giotto came to Padua and started to design the decoration of the chapel, he was faced with a fairly small and very simple architectural shell, on the walls and ceiling of which he had to fit the vast and complex program laid down by the client. In order to do so, he decided to set the *Episodes from the Life of Mary* on the top row, the *Episodes from the Life of Christ* up to the betrayal by Judas on the middle row, and the *Episodes from the Passion* on the lowest level. On the large end wall he placed the *Last Judgment* and on the lower section of the walls, simulating a marble footing, the allegorical figures of the *Virtues* on the right and of the *Vices* on the left. He balanced the displacement caused by the windows on the south wall by setting vertical decorative bands between each of the scenes on the north wall. The end two bands and the middle one extend across the ceiling from the left wall and run down the right one, enclosing the vault and walls in a single frame. The unit of measurement for the individual scenes is determined by the distance between one window and the next and, since the resulting space is fairly limited, the frames that separate the panels horizontally are very low, in order to leave as much spaces as possible for the scene.

The Gospel story is depicted in the sequence that follows.

The Cycle of Paintings in the Chapel

Episodes of Joachim and Ann

1. Joachim Driven from the Temple
2. Joachim Withdraws to Live Among the Shepherds
3. The Announcement to Saint Ann
4. Joachim's Sacrifice
5. Joachim's Dream
6. The Meeting of Joachim and Ann at the Golden Gate

Episodes from the Life of Mary

7. The Birth of Mary
8. The Presentation of Mary in the Temple
9. The Handing Over of the Rods
10. The Prayer for the Flowering of the Rods
11. The Marriage of Mary and Joseph
12. The Bridal Procession of Mary
13. God the Father Instructing the Archangel Gabriel to Make the Announcement to Mary. The Annunciation

Episodes from the Life and Death of Christ

14. The Visitation
15. The Nativity of Jesus
16. The Adoration of the Magi
17. The Presentation of Jesus in the Temple
18. The Flight into Egypt
19. The Slaughter of the Innocents
20. Christ Among the Doctors
21. The Baptism of Christ
22. The Wedding Feast in Cana
23. The Raising of Lazarus
24. Christ's Entry into Jerusalem
25. The Expulsion of the Merchants from the Temple
26. The Betrayal by Judas
27. The Last Supper
28. The Washing of the Feet
29. The Arrest of Christ
30. Christ Before Caiaphas
31. Christ Mocked
32. The Ascent to Calvary
33. The Crucifixion
34. The Lament over the Dead Christ
35. "Noli Me Tangere"
36. The Ascension
37. Pentecost
38. The Two "Coretti"
39. The Last Judgment

The Virtues and Vices

a. Prudence
c. Fortitude
e. Temperance
g. Justice
i. Faith
m. Charity
o. Hope
p. Desperation
n. Envy
l. Faithlessness
h. Injustice
f. Ire
d. Inconstancy
b. Foolishness

1. Joachim Driven from the Temple

Joachim, who had gone to the Temple to sacrifice a lamb, was driven out by the High Priest Ruben since he was still without children (the refusal to procreate was a grave sin in the eyes of the Jews, and sterility a divine punishment). The temple is represented schematically, by two architectural elements: the tabernacle and the pulpit, surrounded by a marble balustrade. The style of the architecture is related to that of Arnolfo di Cambio: it is therefore a clear sign of Giotto's interest in the "modern" architecture of Arnolfo.

2. Joachim Withdraws to Live Among the Shepherds

Joachim, in penance, retires to an isolated place, among the shepherds.
The setting, a mountainous landscape with rocks and trees, fills the entire background of the scene with a naturalistic clarity, in the foliage of the trees and the chiaroscuro of the sheer rock walls, that is entirely absent from the work of Giotto's contemporaries. The naturalistic depiction of animals and plants, something that was already to be seen in the cycle of frescoes depicting *Episodes from the Life of Saint Francis* in the Upper Church of San Francesco in Assisi, achieves a variety and specificity of interpretation that would not be rivaled until the end of the 14th century, in the Paduan miniature of a scientific and naturalistic character.

3. The Announcement to Saint Ann

While Joachim, expelled from the temple, finds refuge among the shepherds, Ann, rapt in prayer in her room, receives the news of her imminent motherhood from the angel. The naturalness of the event is conveyed by means of elements that are credible for their realism: the angel squeezes in through the narrow window; the furnishings of the room, with the details of the drape, the blanket, and the bench cover, give us a clear picture of a 14th-century interior. The portico with a terrace and the staircase leading to it are foreshortened, with an effect of "perspective" already tried out by Giotto in Assisi, but applied with exemplary "scientific" rigor in Padua. The woman spinning under the portico, depicted in a natural pose, is one of the earliest pictorial documents relating to the history of human work.

4. Joachim's Sacrifice

As a sign of purification, Joachim sacrifices a lamb to God on an altar, in an isolated and mountainous setting. The prayer is answered by God, and an angel appears to Joachim to announce this. The symbology of the altar, lamb, praying soul, and blessing hand of God provides a highly effective means, in spite of its concision, of conveying a religious and psychological attitude that is not easy to put into images. Although from a figurative viewpoint, the praying shepherd on the left and angel on the right enclose the scene of Joachim and the altar in the middle, from the symbolic one they indicate that prayer is the way to obtain divine favor. The luminosity of the rocks and clothes, like the naturalism of the flowers and flocks, have a symbolic function, since they are tangible signs of divine grace.

5. Joachim's Dream

Joachim, at the angel's invitation, sets off for home and stops to rest in the shepherds' hut. There, in a dream, the angel announces to him that he is to become a father. Even the shepherds see the angel and a diffuse bright light illuminates the mountains, hut, and clothing. The curled up figure of Joachim is depicted with a naturalism unusual in painting and, even though it has been suggested that the huddling of the limbs and the pyramidal monumentality of the body are derived from the sculptures of Nicola Pisano and Arnolfo di Cambio, it remains one of the most extraordinary conceptions in Italian painting. The clothes are wrapped softly around the body, with a now Gothic elegance in the folds of the drapery.

6. The Meeting of Joachim and Ann at the Golden Gate

According to a tradition that is also recounted in Jacopo da Varazze's *Legenda aurea*, a "golden gate" provided access to the city of Jerusalem. Here Joachim and Ann meet, and kiss. The kiss, as a symbolic act of procreation, is an iconographic tradition of classical origin that survived, with different meanings, into the Middle Ages. The gate, with its classical form of a great arch with two towers, has been associated with the Roman arch in Rimini, and this would provide indirect evidence for a visit by Giotto to Rimini prior to his activity in Padua. The women in Ann's retinue accentuate the narrative and festive character of the scene. The woman with her face half covered by her dark cloak is a symbolic representation of Judaism.

7. The Birth of Mary

The scene is divided into two episodes. Below two women, crouching on the floor of the large room, tend Mary. The older is holding the newborn child in her lap and washing her eyes while the other, younger woman rolls up a piece of cloth. St. Ann, in bed, takes Mary in her arms while other women bring her food and clothing. St. Ann's room is the same, even in the details, as the one in the scene of the angel's apparition, and this is meant to indicate the identity of place, the reality of the episodes depicted. Unlike in the episodes relating to Joachim, the scenes are crowded with figures, onlookers to the events. In fact even in this panel, which follows the ancient tradition of the combined representation of two episodes, the composition and spatial setting of the two women washing Mary are independent and complete in themselves.

8. The Presentation of Mary in the Temple

The temple, similar to the one in the first scene but represented from the opposite side, is set at an angle to the foreground, and therefore to anyone looking at the frescoes in the chapel. Thus Giotto's experimentation with "perspective" proceeds along with the narrative, in an articulation of spaces that is intended to underline the tridimensionality of the real architecture. This is not perspective tackled in mathematical terms, as it would be in the Quattrocento, but a "perspective" based on medieval theorems of optics. Mary and Ann are isolated and their primary role is emphasized by the figures at the edges of the panel. The youth with a basket and the two bystanders, seen from behind, articulate and accentuate the depth of the visual field.

9. The Handing Over of the Rods

The High Priest, by divine inspiration, declares that Mary will marry the man whose rod, offered to the temple, bursts into flower.

The young men, in procession, hand over their rods to the priest. The temple is represented as a building with a nave with a flat ceiling and two aisles. The apse ends in a large arch and hemispherical vault. The definition of space and perspective is as clear and legible as an architectural drawing, and this is an indirect sign that Giotto's architectural interests were extending to Padua.

The gestures are a direct translation of human feelings. While the two youths in the foreground confidently extend their rods toward the priest, Joseph, the last on the left, holds back his rod, as if uncertain whether to hand it over.

10. The Prayer for the Flowering of the Rods

The unity of time and space with the preceding episode is confirmed, as is by now Giotto's usual practice, by the identical representation of the architectural space. The altar-frontal, which is a translation into painting of precious Florentine silk fabrics, is also identical. The semicircular arrangement of the three cloaked figures in the foreground accentuates the depth of the visual field, whereas the figures massed on the left hint at a larger group of praying youths, out of sight. Among these foreshortened figures can be seen the head of Joseph, deliberately set apart to underline the psychological interpretation of his character.

11. The Marriage of Mary and Joseph

The same temple is the setting for the wedding of the very young Mary to Joseph, who is much older than her. In these episodes Giotto follows the tradition of the apocryphal Gospels, in an extremely humane interpretation that is rich in psychological implications and expressed by a highly realistic use of gesture. In this episode Mary's youth is conveyed by her timidly lowered gaze, slender figure, and the naturalness with which the girl places her hand on her belly. St. Joseph gazes at her intensely, conscious of his divine task. The gestures of the young men are also a comment on the event, revealing their wonder but also their disappointment. The young man breaking his rod over his knee became an exemplary figurative scheme, cited even by Raphael in his *Betrothal of the Virgin*.

12. The Bridal Procession of Mary

The central figure of Mary, dressed in white against a blue ground, has such an unmistakably Gothic elegance that it has led some scholars to suggest a visit by Giotto to France. There is no documentary evidence to support this hypothesis, but it is not beyond the bounds of possibility that Giotto may have come into contact with French works of sculpture in ivory. Moreover in Padua he must have seen the portal of Santa Giustina with its great lunette representing the *Ecclesia*, carved, according to the most recent theory, by a French sculptor in the ninth decade of the 12th century. The depiction of the maids is extremely refined, as is that of the three young men playing instruments. In these details Giotto maintains a perfect balance between naturalness and idealization of form.

13. God the Father Instructing the Archangel Gabriel to Make the Announcement to Mary. The Annunciation

The two scenes, although representing two different moments, occupy the whole of the central arch and have preeminence over the remaining scenes because the chapel was dedicated to Our Lady of the Annunciation. This religious festival was celebrated on 25 March of every year, with a sacred representation of the Annunciation: the presence of a great crowd of common people, along with that of the bishop, clergy, and nobility, confirmed the sacredness of the place and, indirectly, the secular power of Enrico Scrovegni. God the Father, seated on a tall throne with cosmatesque ornamentation, addresses Gabriel, while the remaining host of angels looks on. The faces of the angels and the clothes are painted with delicate brush strokes of color, with the Gothic elegance already pointed out in the previous scenes.

In the *Annunciation* Giotto uses the same architectural design to define the space in which the figures of Gabriel and Mary are set. The way in which the two bodies are constructed has a force and majesty that are unprecedented even in Giotto.

Mary, whose face is no longer that of a very young girl, conveys an intense humanity in her gesture of acceptance of the divine will and in the thoughtfulness of her expression. The distinct profile of the face, the form and elegance of the hair gathered into a thick braid, are evident marks of the "classicism" of Giotto's painting. God the Father is painted on a wooden panel, and therefore constitutes an important reference for an understanding of Giotto's methods of painting, at this date, in connection with a different technique from the fresco.

14. The Visitation

Before the birth of Jesus, Mary went to visit her cousin Elizabeth, also pregnant by divine will, although no longer a young woman. The meeting takes place in front of the house, near a porch with elegant columns and a classical frieze. Mary's face is idealized, while Elizabeth's is heavily shaded as an indication of advancing age. Mary's clothes are richly ornamented, as is usual in the iconography of Mary *mater Dei*. The volumetric construction of the bodies is of an extraordinary essentiality and the chromatic relationship of the dresses creates a crescendo of colors that should have been counterbalanced on the right by the blue of the young man's clothing. Only a few traces survive of the blue, a color that can only be applied to a fresco as tempera, so that the underlying drawing and priming are now visible.

15. The Nativity of Jesus

The scene is one of the finest in the whole cycle owing to the quality of the painting and to the treatment of the individual figures. Mary is rising from the pallet to take the infant Jesus in her arms, in line with the Byzantine iconography current in the Middle Ages, and in the same way as she is portrayed in Nicola Pisano's pulpit. Giotto brings new life to these cultural models by approaching the scene realistically: in the way that Mary's body is twisted forward, in the graciousness of the manner in which the woman hands her Jesus, in the foreshortened view of the donkey in the foreground and of the ox in profile. Joseph, viewed from the front, would become one of the figures most frequently used by the imitators of Giotto, as would those of the two shepherds on the right, seen from the back as they are facing toward the angel who is addressing them.

16. The Adoration of the Magi

The wooden shed and the rocky background are a repetition with slight variations of those in the preceding scene. Mary holds out Jesus to the kneeling king, in accordance with an iconography that was very common in the wooden sculptures portraying *Mary Holding the Child on Her Knee* of the Romanesque era. The angel on the right is holding the king's gift, a precious gold reliquary. The majesty of the scene has its ideal fulcrum in the Child, who is also the center of the diagonal that extends in perspective from the king's feet to the top of the rock in the right-hand corner. The two camels on the left are painted with extreme naturalism. The face of the youth holding them back is also very beautiful, and is depicted from a worm's-eye view that conveys the height and power of the two camels.

17. The Presentation of Jesus in the Temple

The space is defined by the elegant canopy above the altar. On the right stands the prophetess Anna with the prophetic scroll; alongside her the prophet Simeon hands the Child to Mary. On the left-hand side of the scene, after Mary, can be seen Joseph, with the two doves to be offered to the temple, and a young woman holding a candle. In the simplicity of the composition, Mary's attitude assumes an emotional clarity and a narrative sincerity of great humanity. As the scenes progress the color of the clothes becomes increasingly blurred in the chiaroscuro of the folds. Here the clothing of the young woman and of Simeon's cloak change color in a way not to be seen in the earlier scenes. The delicate skin of the Child is effectively rendered by brush strokes of a liquid transparency.

18. The Flight into Egypt

The composition of this scene is one of the most beautiful in the cycle. The pyramidal form of Mary and the Child is echoed in the shape of the rock behind, so that psychological attitude and pictorial form are combined in the isolation of Mary. St. Joseph and the young men accompanying the Holy Family are placed at the edges of the scene, in the background. This composition was used again by Giotto's collaborators in Assisi, in the cycle of frescoes in the right-hand transept of the Lower Church, and, in the Quattrocento and Cinquecento, by the Paduan painters who frescoed the school of San Giuseppe in that city.

19. The Slaughter of the Innocents

King Herod appears at a loggia to order the massacre of the children. A building on an octagonal plan in the background, identified by some scholars with the church of San Francesco in Bologna, alludes symbolically to the martyrdom and beatitude of the Holy Innocents. The climax of the tragic event is entrusted to the figure of the executioner in the center, caught in the act of lifting the sword with which he is going to impale the child clinging to its mother's body. The face of the hooded man also reveals the brutality of the killing. A contrast to the anguish of the group of women on the right is provided on the left by the horrified retreat of the soldiers from the sight of the pile of tiny bodies heaped on the ground. This is one of the most intense of Giotto's paintings.

20. Christ Among the Doctors

It is not just the apse of the temple where Jesus is talking to the doctors of the Holy Scriptures that is depicted, but also the aisles with cross vaults and the large central hall. Thus the architectural space in this episode is very complex and shows the progress that Giotto was making in his investigation of perspective. The panel was detached during the last century, and as a result the surface of the painting has been abraded in many parts or its colors altered. Giotto's effort to depict the figures of the doctors seated on the benches at the sides in "perspective" is interesting. In order to vary their arrangement, the painter shifts the figure of Christ slightly to the right and spreads the five doctors on the left fairly widely. The five on the right, on the other hand, are set closer together, in a more rigid pattern.

21. The Baptism of Christ

Jesus is baptized in the Jordan by St. John the Baptist. God the Father sends down the dove of the Holy Ghost to his Son.

The mystery of the Holy Trinity, expressed in this scene representing the Gospel story, is depicted with splendid details. God the Father is shown with a highly effective foreshortening from below, while the body of Christ and the water of the river are painted with a fluidity that achieves an extraordinary realism. The pink clothing of the Baptist, like that of the angels, has a lightness of color that is only partially evident in the preceding scenes.

22. The Wedding Feast in Cana

The wedding is set in a space surrounded by walls with a loggia, resembling the courtyard of a noble residence. The walls are partly covered, in the manner of a tapestry, by a piece of striped cloth, evidently a 14th-century custom. The tablecloth, glasses, and amphorae are also from Giotto's time.

The location of the table in a corner creates a great deal of room for the servants and guests. Particular emphasis is given to the miracle at the moment in which the water poured into the amphorae turns into wine.

The fat man tasting the miraculous drink introduces a note of gaiety, while the dignified elegance of the bride, alone at the center, responds fully to Giotto's ideal of feminine beauty.

23. The Raising of Lazarus

The use of the rocky backdrop as a geometrical framework on which to arrange the figures—already tried out in the *Flight into Egypt*—constantly recurs in Giotto's work. In this scene the triangular profile of the mountain forms a diagonal division between two sections: on the left the empty space of blue sky in which stands, in isolation, Christ with his hand raised in blessing to restore Lazarus to life; on the right Lazarus, still wrapped in bandages, is surrounded by the crowd. In the lower part, in the foreground, Mary and Martha are kneeling in prayer, and in the corner on the right two youths hold up the marble slab of the tomb. This last, highly expressive figure, would be reutilized in the Padua Baptistry by Giusti de' Menabuoi (*c.* 1376), whose panel depicting the *Miracles of Christ* can be seen as an explicit homage to Giotto.

24. Christ's Entry into Jerusalem

In this episode the gesture of spreading mantles at Christ's feet is depicted in progression: the man on the right in the act of removing his arm from the sleeve, the boy about to free his hands and head from the mantle, the kneeling youth who has already spread his on the ground... As in the previous episode, Peter and John stand out from the group of Apostles, but with them, for the first time, is an Apostle with a beard and flowing locks, an unusually forceful expression on his face, and a body of majestic frame, who will reappear in the following scenes. The boy climbing the olive tree is a variation on the one in the tree in the *Lamentation of the Poor Clares* in the Franciscan cycle of Assisi, just as the kneeling boy recalls the figure of the youth in the *Miracle of the Spring*.

25. The Expulsion of the Merchants from the Temple

The front of the temple has an elegant porch with a ceiling of crossed vaulting cells, represented at an angle to accentuate the depth of field. The same function is performed by the tympanum that, cut in half, hints at its continuation beyond the frame that encloses the scene. The rosettes that decorate the tympana of the portico's facade are classical in style. The two equestrian statues in the middle have been linked to the horses of St. Mark's in Venice. Even the two lions are regarded as a citation from the lion in Piazzetta San Marco. In this scene the central figure of Christ represents the climax of the psychological and moral tension of the Gospel story, then reflected, deliberately, in the figures of a child with a dove and another who is seeking refuge from the divine rage by clinging to John, who protects him and cries.

26. The Betrayal by Judas

Here Giotto relies on the gazes and the hands of his figures to tell the story. Judas is painted in profile, with disagreeable features and his left hand clutching the bag of thirty pieces of gold. The priest who has handed it to him stares at him fixedly, making a reassuring gesture. The priest on the right is pointing his thumb toward Judas, the person who will carry out the betrayal. The composition is intentionally static, to indicate the fatality of the event. The devil holds onto Judas, as in folk versions of the tale; Giotto will introduce elements of folk tradition into the *Last Judgment* as well.

27. The Last Supper

The view at an angle, already used in previous scenes, finds a rigorous application in the elegant loggia depicted in this panel. The two very slender columns in the foreground delimit the space beyond which stand the bench and the table spread with the supper. The Apostles are arranged in this geometrically measurable space: the ones in the foreground have their backs turned while those seated along the back wall are seen from the front. The sky above the roof of the loggia lends credibility to the composition, as do the windows—one closed and the other half-open—in the rear wall of the room. Thus the regular arrangement of the twelve Apostles around the table is based on a geometrical pattern, and one that is easy to grasp if this composition at an angle is compared with the less carefully gauged one of *Christ Among the Doctors*.

28. The Washing of the Feet

In the same room Christ washes the feet of the Apostles standing around him, absorbed in thought. All are portrayed except Judas, of whom we can only see the halo. The naturalness of Peter's gesture as he lifts his robe to allow Christ to wash his foot is exemplary, an unmistakable sign of the humanity of Christ and of the interpretation that should be made of the Gospel texts, according to the example set by St. Francis. Giotto translates into painting the religious and secular values of his time in a manner comprehensible to all, but especially to the common people. Even the Apostle lacing his shoes and John holding a jug in his hand are not merely gestures of great realistic immediacy, but also express an idealized stillness, in a perfect balance between humanity and holiness.

29. The Arrest of Christ

Judas embraces Christ and, covering him with his cloak, forms a single central block. The device of this block, the yellow cloak that covers both figures, and the extreme closeness of the two profiles and of the eyes staring intensely into each other create the sense of drama, of the event that is about to take place. The size of the throng of soldiers can be reckoned from the dense mass of helmets, and especially from the spears, lamps, and staffs outlined against the sky. The evocative force of this thicket of spears against the blue sky was to influence Altichiero in his *Decapitation of Saint George* (chapel of San Giorgio in Il Santo). From this panel, he also took the hooded figure viewed from behind, and above all the paratactic construction of the figures.

30. Christ Before Caiaphas

The scene is set inside a room formed by a cubic "box" open at the front and aligned with the frame of the panel. The "perspective" is provided by the ceiling of the room, the beams, and the capitals in the corners. All the figures are located in an almost continuous foreground: Caiaphas is rending his clothes; a priest is instructing a soldier to lead Christ to the tribunal; Christ turns toward the soldier who is threatening him with a raised hand. The idealization of his features, the slight curve of his shoulders, and the peacefulness of his gaze make the figure of Christ one of the most moving in the cycle. The soldiers are dressed in clothing richly ornamented with golden embroidery, as are the borders of the priests' robes. In this Giotto was falling into line with a Gothic taste that held sway in the courts of northern Italy during 14th century.

31. Christ Mocked

Christ, clothed in a royal mantle, is mocked and scourged. He is encircled by his tormentors, while one of them, a young Negro dressed in white, stands slightly apart and forms the fulcrum of the scene. On the right Pilate and two priests comment upon the event.
The use of violet and a range of browns in this episode is very refined; the way that the white of the clothing worn by the Negro in the center shades into gray and the pink of the priest's cloak changes into violet is splendid. The scourging takes place in the open, in the inner court of a building; there is a foreshortened view of a facade with windows.
The elegant trabeation of the pergola has a classical ornamentation of palmettes and two crouching lions, reminiscent of Giotto's Roman activity.

32. The Ascent to Calvary

From the gate of Jerusalem—the same as the one depicted in *Christ's Entry into Jerusalem* —emerge a group of devout women who are following the soldiers and priests to Mount Calvary. Mary is pushed back by a soldier and Christ turns to look at her. The scene centers on the sorrowful expression of the Madonna and that of the face of Christ, as tender in its divine suffering as we saw it in the scene of *Christ Before Caiaphas*. The slow progress of Christ, bent under the weight of the cross, is accentuated by the figure's isolation against the blue ground. The movement of the scene, on the other hand, is conveyed by the two figures of young men preceding Christ. This painting, like the one below it depicting *Christ Among the Doctors*, was detached in the 19th century and is in very poor condition as a result.

33. The Crucifixion

The cross stands out against a blue ground; around it circle the mourning angels. The impression of circularity is created by a daring foreshortening of the two angels above the cross and by the way that the ones at the side are depicted in perspective at an angle. In the foreground on the right, soldiers argue over Christ's clothing; behind them stands the centurion Longinus. In the right-hand corner, a beautiful face of a youth, very similar to the one on the right of Pilate in the scene of *Christ Mocked*. To the left of the cross is the group made up of Mary supported by John and a devout woman. Kneeling at the foot of the cross, Mary Magdalen weeps and dries the Savior's feet with her hair. Christ's body, painted with a very light touch, is an extraordinary piece of work.

34. The Lament over the Dead Christ

The drama of the *Passion of Christ* reaches its climax in this scene. The "lament" is a recurrent theme in the sculptural groups of the Romanesque period, but Giotto interprets it with a pathos that cannot be found, for example, in the sculpture of Giovanni Pisano or Jacopone da Todi's "lauda." The eyes of all the mourners are turned on Mary, who is holding the dead body of Christ in her lap, with her face against that of her Son. Devout women support his head and hands, Mary Magdalen his feet. All the varieties of sorrow are depicted: the restrained expressions of Nicodemus and Joseph of Arimethea, on the right-hand side; the famous one of John who is spreading his arms behind him, echoed by one of the devout women on the left side; the mute one of the two huddled devout women seen from the back.

35. "Noli Me Tangere"

The narration of the scene is split into two sections. In the first, on the left, two angels are seated on the tomb from which Christ has already risen. In the second, on the right, Christ meets Mary Magdalen and, although moving away from her, invites her to tell the Apostles that he has risen. Mary Magdalen's timorous stretching of her hands toward Christ and the Savior's slight shrinking away represent one of the most intense passages in Italian painting. The colors have a symbolic function and an extraordinary luminosity, as do the tunics of the angels and the marble of the tomb. The sleeping faces of the latter are painted with broad brush strokes and a blend of colors that we see here for the first time in Padua, but that were to become the dominant style of Giotto's closest collaborators working in the Lower Church of San Francesco in Assisi.

36. The Ascension

At the bottom Mary and the Apostles, on a rocky height, gaze up toward Christ ascending into heaven. The bright light softly enfolds the Savior's body, stretched in the movement of ascent and with the hands already outside the field of vision bounded by the frame. In an effort to create a realistic effect of tridimensionality, Giotto sets two angels pointing to Christ in the background. The lightness of his figure is contrasted, figuratively as well, by the solidity of form given to the bodies of Mary and the Apostles, some of whom are recognizable through the repetition of their faces and clothing: not only Peter and John, but also the Apostle with the sumptuous robes and the one with flowing beard and hair, are identical with the figures in the *Washing of the Feet*.

37. Pentecost

In this last scene, new elements are again to be found in the "perspective" treatment of space. The elegant Gothic shrine in which the Apostles are seated is represented not only at an angle, but also with the elements of its architecture in the foreground: this produces a clear separation between the observer and the cubic "box" in which the scene is set. Even the Apostles arranged in such a geometrically defined space is much better constructed than in the *Last Supper*. The light shining on the Apostles bestows on their clothing a soft chromaticity that is unprecedented in this cycle. From this experience Giotto and his studio would retain the sense of a new relationship between form and color; in the paintings in Assisi they would take up where they left off in the final scenes of the Paduan cycle.

38. The Two "Coretti"

In these two painted works of architecture Giotto's experiments with "perspective" reach the most advanced level attained by the whole of painting in the Trecento. We do not know how and why Giotto came to tackle the question, which was to become a fundamental problem in the painting of the Quattrocento, with so much insight in Padua. It is certain that Paduan cultural circles (a number of lecturers from the local university had frequent contacts with the universities of Paris and Bologna) could have stimulated Giotto's interest in optics, and especially in the three-dimensional representation of reality. In this case the two spaces with their pointed arches open up and "break through" the wall. The cross vaults, painted illusionistically between the two arches, simulate a transept intersecting the nave; this accords with the model of the chapel that Enrico Scrovegni is offering to the Virgin in the fresco on the facade. We are therefore led to suppose that Giotto painted the chapel with a transept in the *Last Judgment* because the original design had been altered over the course of the chapel's construction; the artist compensated for this change by depicting the transept that had not been built.

39. The Last Judgment

The *Last Judgment* takes up the entire end wall of the chapel. Christ the Judge is seated in a mandorla at the top, supported by the symbols of the four Evangelists; with his right hand the Savior is welcoming the blessed souls, while rejecting the reprobates with his left. Cherubim and seraphim support the mandorla and sound the trumpets of God, while hosts of angels are arranged symmetrically at the sides of the great three-mullioned window. Alongside Christ, the apostles are seated on marble thrones resting on a semicircular dais. Beneath them and to the left of the Savior, a river of fire runs down from the mandorla, carrying away the damned and casting them down toward the monstrous figure of Lucifer. To Christ's right, the host of saints, headed by the Madonna, makes its way upward, while that of the blessed souls, led by angels, approaches the great Cross. Beneath the latter, supported by two angels, the Madonna flanked by Saints John and Catherine welcome Enrico Scrovegni as he offers her the model of the chapel, supported by a churchman. Further down the souls of the blessed are rising from their tombs. His didactic intentions induced the artist to make the

composition schematic; nonetheless the large scene is rich in coloristic and formal values that are wholly in keeping with Giotto's brilliance of conception. The pictorial representation of the Apostles and Christ appears to be closely related to that of the scenes on the walls; the same can be said of the Madonna and the angels. The figure of Enrico, kneeling in front of the Madonna, is splendid: here, for the first time and in contravention of the medieval tradition, Giotto has depicted the client on the same scale as the Madonna and saints.

The work of Giotto's studio has been identified in the group of the blessed (tradition has it that the artist portrayed himself among them) and especially in the damned. The conception of these two areas of the painting—though marked by a falling off in style—can still be ascribed to Giotto, owing to the variety of attitudes and forms to be found in them.

The same can be said of the depiction of the angelic hosts; note, for example, the complex foreshortening of their haloes and faces.

The churchman supporting the chapel has recently been identified, although only hypothetically, as Altegrado de' Cattanei, canon of the cathedral and friend of Enrico Scrovegni, who was appointed bishop in 1303.

The group of blessed souls and some parts of the hell are badly damaged.

The Virtues and Vices

Proceeding from the apse toward the *Last Judgment* we find, painted in monochrome, the *Virtues* on the side of Heaven and, opposite them, the *Vices* on the side of Hell. The *Virtues and Vices*, set inside very deep niches of marble, are recognizable by their characteristic symbology. The name of the Virtue or Vice is inscribed on the lintel of the marble wall; another inscription on the base of the marble niche describes the specific character of each figure.

Although enclosed within a limited space, the figures are painted in a great variety of attitudes. The handling of some of the details can be said to be among the greatest achievements of 14th-century painting. The vase with flowers and fruit held by *Charity* is the earliest example of a still life, while the frieze depicting a dance in the painting of *Justice* is one of the first examples of a representation of that bourgeois culture that would be so extensively depicted by Ambrogio Lorenzetti in the famous fresco of *Good Government* in the City Hall of Siena.

Hope takes flight toward the angel who is holding out a crown to her; *Desperation* is represented by a hanged woman—symbol of suicide—whose soul is being torn out by a demon to be carried off to hell.

Charity is standing on sacks of money, for only spiritual wealth makes it possible to gain divine favor. She is contrasted not by Avarice but by *Envy*, clutching a bag of money in her left hand and trying to seize another with her right. Emerging from the mouth of the ugly old woman, who has big ears and horns, is a serpent that turns to strike her. In the end Envy is like a fire that cannot be extinguished.

Faith stands firm, holding the scroll of Revealed Truth and

Prudence

Fortitude

Foolishness

Inconstancy

Temperance   Justice   Faith

Ire   Injustice   Faithlessness

the processional cross with which she has destroyed the pagan idols, false scriptures, and cabbalistic texts at her feet. *Faithlessness*, or *Idolatry*, is totally fascinated by the idol (the statuette of a woman in her hand) and turns her back, heedless of the texts read out by the Prophet, whose figure extends the frame above. *Justice*—represented as a queen on a throne, as befits the most important of the cardinal virtues—is holding a balance. A good act is being performed on the right-hand pan, a bad one on the left. The frieze underneath depicts civilized life under good government: hunting, dancing, travel. *Injustice*, on the other hand, is represented by a warrior with a castle in the background. Under bad government grow the trees of evil: war, crime, pillage.

Temperance is depicted with a bit in her mouth and blindfolded, to signify that she curbs her impulses and makes no distinctions. By contrast, *Ire* shows her violence by tearing apart her dress at the breast, that echoes the gesture of Caiaphas in the Gospel scene. *Fortitude* is an imposing figure, her head covered by a lion skin; her right hand grips a club, her left holds a shield emblazoned with a lion. *Inconstancy* is depicted as a young woman who, seated on a wheel, is about to fall backwards, even though trying to keep her balance by spreading her arms. *Prudence* is reflected in a mirror as she writes in a book. The dual image, the two faces, are meant to signify that past experience provides a guide for the present (the book is a metaphor for memory). *Foolishness* is the ungainly figure of a buffoon equipped with a gnarled stick and crowned with feathers, a symbol of that fatuous levity that so often turns into an offence to other people's sensitivities.

Charity

Hope

Envy

Desperation

The Vault and the Figured Frames

When Giotto planned the iconographic distribution of the whole cycle of pictures, the apse, which was originally intended to have a transept, cannot have been completely finished, since only the nave was decorated. In his arrangement of the scenes, the artist had to take into account the fact that there were no openings in the side wall on the left, while the one on the right had windows of considerable size. He compensated for the difference between the two walls by devising broad frames that formed a structure within which the scenes could be set. In these frames, ornamented with Roman plant and cosmatesque motifs, Giotto inserted a number of half-length figures, in accordance with a specific iconography. On the vaulted ceiling he painted the *Vault of Heaven*, divided into two sections. In the first, adjacent to the *Last Judgment*, medallions contain half-length portraits of the *Madonna and Child with the Prophets* who had foretold the divine maternity of Mary: Malachi, Baruch, Isaiah, and Daniel hold the scrolls of their prophecies. In the second section, again inside medallions, are portrayed *Christ and the Four Prophets* who predicted his birth: John the Baptist, Ezekiel, Jeremiah, and Micah. The frames that separate the two sections are decorated with geometric motifs and enclose in turn multifoiled frames containing half-length portraits of Mary's forebears, all kings, patriarchs, and judges, according to the genealogy of the Old and New Testaments. On the walls, the frames in the top row contain the *Apostles*. At the ends of the middle row are the four female saints *Catherine of Alexandria*, *Margaret of Antioch*, *Lucy*, and *Elizabeth of Hungary*. At the ends of the lower row, we

find the *Four Evangelists* (Matthew, Mark, Luke, and John) and the *Four Doctors of the Church* (Gregory the Great, Jerome, Ambrose, and Augustine).

In the remaining bands—i.e. in the painted frames on the left-hand wall that separate the scenes in the middle and upper rows—are depicted episodes from the Old Testament that are correlated with the adjacent Gospel scene, establishing a close connection between the story from the New Testament and the Old Testament one that prefigures it. The episodes are: *The Circumcision, Moses Causes Water to Gush from the Rock, The Creation of Adam, The Sons of the Prophets of Jericho Go to Meet the Prophet Elisha, The Archangel Michael Fighting the Dragon, Moses Raising the Serpent on the Cross, Moses Receiving the Tables of the Law, Jonah Swallowed by the Whale, Judah Son of Jacob, Elijah Borne off by the Chariot of Fire*, and *God Consigns a Scroll to the Prophet Ezekiel*. It has been suggested that Giotto's collaborators, including the "Master of San Nicola," were responsible for these half-length figures in frames. For such an extensive and demanding work, Giotto undoubtedly relied on the assistance of his students; but his supervision must have been constant, for these paintings display the same soft blend of colors that can be seen in the large scenes on the walls. They must have been executed, as was the usual practice, from top to bottom, however using a fully constructed scaffolding covering the entire field to be frescoed: in fact the spreading of the paint on the ceiling is just like that of the last scenes at the bottom. The *Madonna and Child*—now in poor condition as it was detached, along with the tondi depicting Prophets to its right

during the Second World War—can surely be attributed to Giotto owing to its monumentality of form and handling of color; the same can be said of the figure of Christ, the remaining Prophets, and the Apostles. The episodes from the Old Testament that were certainly painted by the master himself are the ones depicting *Jonah Swallowed by the Whale* and the *Creation of Adam*; in others, such as *Moses Receiving the Tables of the Law* or *The Archangel Michael Fighting the Dragon*, the flat use of paint and the thin line surrounding the figures suggests the work of a collaborator. Yet these are still very marginal interventions and executed under the close supervision of Giotto, who in this Paduan cycle realized the best preserved work of his artistic maturity.

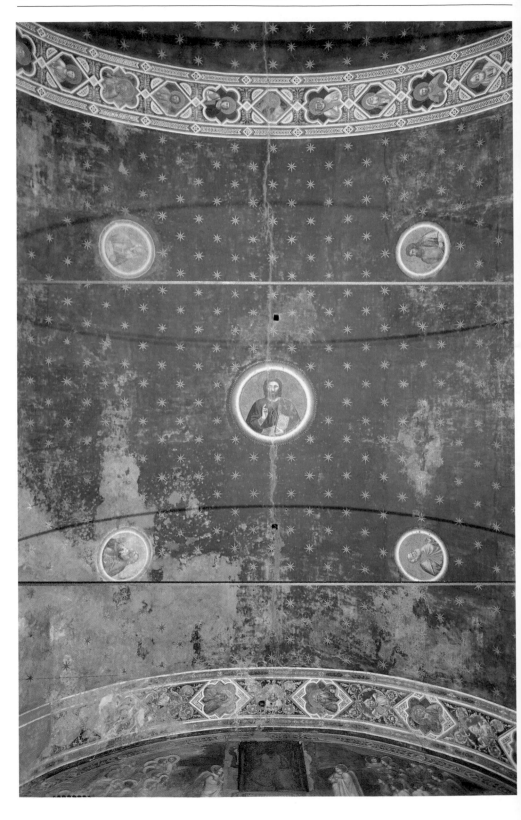

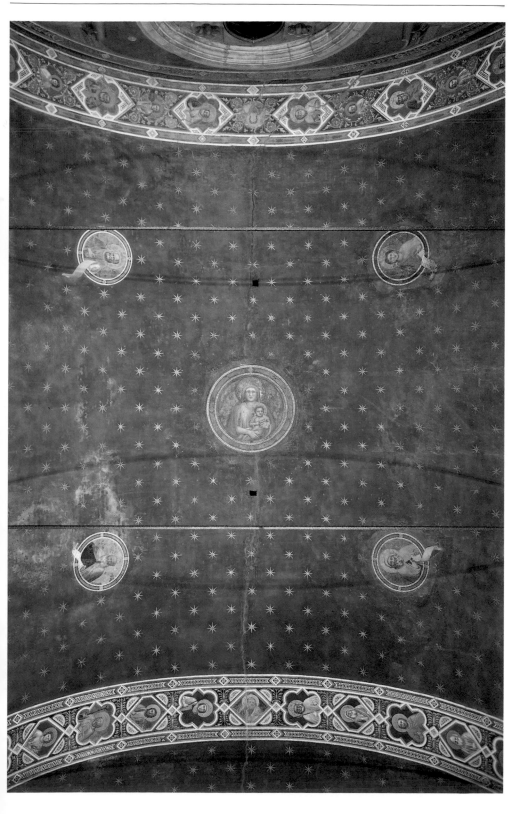

The Crucifix

The great *Crucifix* painted by Giotto for the Scrovegni Chapel, which Cavalcaselle saw on the rear wall above the sarcophagus of Enrico, is now in the Museo Civico. It is painted on both sides: *Christ Between the Madonna and Saint John* on the front, the *Symbols of the Four Evangelists* and the *Lamb of God* on the back. Originally, therefore, it was not hung on the wall, but supported by a *pergula*, as was the custom in the 14th century. This base may have been located under the triumphal arch or, as is more likely, halfway along the nave where the two ambones and the two altars dedicated to St. John the Baptist and Saint Catherine are located.

Some scholars attribute the work to Giotto's studio, others attribute it to the second period of the master's activity in Padua.

Stylistic parallels with the panel painting of *God the Father* on the arch and with the *Crucifixion* frescoed on the left wall provide evidence in support of the latter hypothesis.

Frescoes, Sculptures and Ornaments in the Apse and Sacristy

The Frescoes on the Walls of the Apse

After Giotto's departure from Padua, the walls of the apse still had to be frescoed. The decoration was completed by an anonymous pupil of Giotto's—known as the "Master of the Scrovegni Choir"—with the last episodes from the life of Mary: the *Death*, the *Funeral*, the *Assumption*, and the *Coronation*.

The anonymous artist took from Giotto the monumental depiction of the figures, the range of colors, and the typology of faces, while his approach to narration was more impassioned and expressionistic.

The spreading of the paint is firmer and devoid of the patterns of light and shade typical of Giotto and his close collaborators; as a consequence the tones are more somber, without the luminosity that is characteristic of the scenes in the nave. Nor is the arrangement of the composition influenced by the concern with "perspective" displayed by Giotto: it is based on a paratactic disposition of the figures and shows not the slightest sign of an attempt at "perspective."

The Sculptures of Giovanni Pisano

On the altar of the apse stand three pieces of marble sculpture inscribed with the words IOH.IS MAGISTRI NICOLI.

In this work, therefore, Giovanni Pisano signed himself as the son of the sculptor Nicola, who was highly esteemed by Giotto, and it is not beyond the bounds of possibility that Giotto recommended the work of the Pisano family to Enrico Scrovegni.

The *Madonna* can be considered one of Giovanni's masterpieces owing to the softness of the modeling, the Gothic elegance of the spreading clothes, and the expressive intensity with which the Madonna and Child are looking at one another. The two *Candle-holding Angels* are also signed by Giovanni, executed in ca. 1305, when the chapel was consecrated.

The Tomb and Statue of Enrico Scrovegni

On 22 March 1336 Enrico Scrovegni, in exile in Venice, dictated his will, in which he expressed the desire to be buried in Padua, in the chapel that he had built by the grace of God and at his own expense. He died on 20 August. On 23 November his remains, temporarily buried in San Mattia on Murano, were transported to Padua. The burial urn must have been placed *in situ* before 1320, the year in which Enrico left the city to seek asylum in Venice; however the slab with the figure lying on top of the tomb was executed after his death. If compared with the slab on the tomb, the features of the sculpture of Enrico set in a niche in the sacristy reveal a certain difference in age: perhaps the work, dates from the years prior to his exile. The two sculptures have at times been attributed to Giovanni Pisano, at times to his studio, and at still others to an anonymous Tuscan. Wolters attributes both works to the Venetian sculptor responsible for the sepulchral monument to Castellano Salomone in the Treviso Cathedral.

Ornaments, Vestments, and Frescoes in the Apse and Sacristy

Along with the *Crucifix*, Scrovegni had provided the chapel with ornaments and vestments. Unfortunately nothing remains of the original 14th-century paraments, liturgical books, and vestments. The sacristy contains a large *cabinet* from this period and a fresco decoration on the walls dating from around the middle of the Trecento. The chapel *bell*, mentioned in the document of 1305, is now kept in the museum. The wooden stalls in the nave were installed in the 16th century. Between the *14th-century wooden stalls* in the apse there are two paintings of the same subject, the *Madonna and Child*: one can be attributed to Giusto de' Menabuoi, the other to Jacopo da Verona.

Giovanni Pisano, Virgin and Child.

Restorations of the Chapel

In Giovanni Valle's plan of Padua (1784), the chapel and house of the Scrovegni family are drawn as neighboring but not adjoining buildings. This is a clear sign that the drawing by Marino Urbani of the facade of the Palazzo Scrovegni contains a number of alterations of a scenographic character. In Urbani's drawing the chapel has a 15th-century porch that collapsed in 1817, as we are told by Giannantonio Moschini. But the house itself must have been in a highly advanced state of decay as it was demolished in 1827 to make room for a modest habitation.

During the 18th century the *Announcing Angel* and the *Annunziata* had been painted on the facade, at the sides of the three-mullioned window, with two figures of *Saints* underneath—as seen in the Naya photographs taken in 1867.

Inside the chapel, the area of the apse contained an altar, perhaps dating from the late Cinquecento, that was removed during the 19th-century restorations. The chapel, whose ownership had passed from the Scrovegni family to the Foscari-Gradenigo family, was purchased by the Commune of Padua in 1880, for the sum of 54,971 lire.

The deterioration of the frescoes, pointed out by Rumohr ("The painting is in a very sad condition ... since the frescoes have been washed by a clumsy hand and then repainted in tempera"), was recognized as a problem requiring urgent attention by Pietro Selvatico. Giovanni Battista Cavalcaselle took part in the work of the commission and when he was in Padua (1857, 1864, 1865) studied Giotto's frescoes, making drawings from them. In the years 1865-67 all of Giotto's frescoes were photographed by the Naya firm of Venice and scale drawings were made of each panel by Augusto Caratti and Leopoldo Toniolo, with annotations on the damage to every single scene. The restoration was entrusted in 1869-71 to Guglielmo Botti of Pisa and then, in 1881-94, to Antonio Bertolli of Padua. After the Second World War there was a long debate over the need to do something about the frescoes. During the war itself, a system of protection had been set up with sandbags and tondi depicting the *Madonna and Child* and three *Prophets* had been removed from the ceiling. The thick layer of dust that had settled on the frescoes during the war had reduced their legibility, and in some places the plaster and the film of paint had begun to lift off, especially in the areas around the truss rods. The preliminary work on the walls, carried out from 1961 to 1963, involved the replacement of four of the five truss rods and substitution of metal trusses for the wooden ones. Over the same period, Giotto's frescoes were restored by Leonetto Tintori.

During subsequent checks the blame for the deterioration of the frescoes has been ascribed not to the usual causes, but to atmospheric pollution. More recent damage, although fortunately only partial and confined to the decorative fascia of the vault adjacent to the facade, was caused by the earthquake of 1976. The work of restoration has been carried out by the Istituto Centrale per il Restauro. The last general review of the conditions of the fresco, undertaken in 1989 by the same body, was completed in 1991.

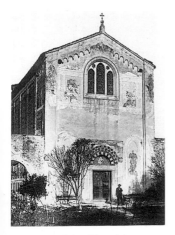

Exterior of the Chapel in a 1867 photograph.

Bibliography

J.A. Crowe, G.B. Cavalcaselle, *A New History of Painting in Italy*, vol. I, London 1864.

A. Tolomei, "La Cappella degli Scrovegni all'Arena di Padova," in *Scritti vari*, Padua 1880.

A. Tolomei, *La chiesa di Santa Maria della Carità dipinta da Giotto*, Padua 1880.

H. Thode, *Franz von Assisi und die Anfanger der Kunst der Renaissance in Italien*, Berlin 1885.

J.A. Crowe, G.B. Cavalcaselle, *Storia della Pittura in Italia*, 2nd ed., vol. I, Florence 1886.

H. Thode, *Giotto*, Bielefeld-Leipzig 1899.

B. Berenson, *The Florentine Painters of the Renaissance*, New York-London 1896 (2nd ed. 1900, 3rd ed. 1909).

A. Venturi, *Storia dell'Arte Italiana*, vol. V, *La Pittura del Trecento e le sue origini*, Milan 1907.

F. Rintelen, *Giotto und die Giotto-Apokryphen*, Munich-Leipzig 1912.

A. Moschetti, "La distrutta iconostasi alla cappella Scrovegni," in *Atti e Memorie dell'Accademia di SS.LL.AA. di Padova*, XXXIX, Padua 1922-23.

R. van Marie, *The Development of the Italian Schools of Painting*, vol. III, The Hague 1924.

W. Suida, "Giottos Stil," in *Festschrift zum 60. Geburtstag von Paul Clemen*, Düsseldorf-Bonn 1926, pp. 335-37.

P. Toesca, *Storia dell'Arte italiana. Il Medioevo*, vol. II, Turin 1927.

O. Ronchi, "Un documento inedito del 9 gennaio 1305 intorno alla Cappella degli Scrovegni," in *Atti e Memorie dell'Accademia di SS.LL.AA. di Padova*, vol. LII, t. II, Padua 1935-36, pp. 205-11.

R. Salvini, *Giotto. Bibliografia*, Rome 1938.

R. Offner, "Giotto, non Giotto," in *The Burlington Magazine*, LXXIV, 1939, pp. 259-68; LXXV, 1940, pp. 96-113.

L. Coletti, *I primitivi dall'arte benedettina a Giotto*, vol. I, Novara 1941.

P. Toesca, *Giotto*, Turin 1941.

R. Oertel, "Wende der Giotto-Vorschung," in *Zeitschrift für Kunstgeschichte*, XI, 1943-44, pp. 1-27.

R. Gallo, "Contributi alla storia della scultura veneziana. Andreolo de' Santi," in *Archivio Veneto*, series V, vol. XLIV, 1949.

P. Toesca, *Il Trecento*, Turin 1951.

R. Longhi, "Giotto spazioso," in *Paragone*, no. 31, 1952, pp. 18-24.

R. Oertel, *Die Frühzeit der Italienische Malerei*, Stuttgart 1953 (2nd ed. 1966).

A. Chastel, *L'Art italien*, Paris 1956.

R. Offner, *A Critical and Historical Corpus of Florentine Painting*, sect. III, vol. VI, New York 1956.

C. Gnudi, "Il passo di Riccobaldo Ferrarese relativo a Giotto e il problema della sua autenticità," in *Studies in the History of Art Dedicated to William E. Suida*, London 1957, pp. 26-30.

U. Schlegel, "Zum Bildprogramm der Arena-Kapelle," in *Zeitschrift für Kunstgeschichte*, 1957.

C. Gnudi, "Giotto," in *Enciclopedia Universale dell'Arte Italiana*, vol. VI, Venice-Rome 1958, pp. 219-39.

C. Gnudi, *Giotto*, Milan 1959.

M. Meiss, *Giotto and Assisi*, New York 1960 (repr. 1967).

A. Prosdocimi, "Il Comune di Padova e la Cappella degli Scrovegni nell'Ottocento," in *Bollettino del Museo Civico di Padova*, year XLIX, no. I, 1960.

R. Salvini, *Tutta la pittura di Giotto*, Milan 1962.

L. Tintori, M. Meiss, *The Painting of the Life of St. Francis in Assisi*, New York 1962.

D. Gioseffi, *Giotto architetto*, Milan 1963.

C. Bellinati, "La Cappella degli Scrovegni di Giotto all'Arena (1300-1306)," in *Giotto e la sua provincia*, nos. 11-12, 1967.

G. Previtali, *Giotto e la sua bottega*, Milan 1967 (2nd ed. 1974).

F. Flores d'Arcais, "Affreschi giotteschi nella Basilica del Santo a Padova," in *Critica d'Arte*, no. 97, 1968, pp. 23-33.

L. Mack Bongiorno, "The

Theme of the Old and New Law in the Arena Chapel," in *The Art Bulletin*, no. I, 1968, pp. 11-20.

F. Bologna, *Novità su Giotto. Giotto al tempo della cappella Peruzzi*, Turin 1969.

R. Salvini, C. De Benedetti, *Giotto. Bibliografia*, Rome 1970.

G. Palumbo, *Giotto e i giotteschi in Assisi*, Rome 1969.

F. Zuliani, "Per la diffusione del giottismo nelle Venezie e in Friuli: gli affreschi dell'Abbazia di Sesto al Reghena," in *Arte Veneta*, XXIV, 1970.

C. Bellinati, "Il Giudizio Universale nella cappella di Giotto all'Arena," in *Patavinum*, no. 1, 1971.

C. Bellinati, "Ricerche storiche nella cappella degli Scrovegni," in *Patavinum*, no. 2, 1971.

C. Gnudi, "Sugli inizi di Giotto e i suoi rapporti col mondo gotico," in *Giotto e il suo tempo. Atti del Congresso internazionale per il VII centenario della nascita di Giotto (1967)*, Rome 1971.

A. Prosdocimi, "Osservazioni sulla partitura delle scene affrescate da Giotto nella Cappella degli Scrovegni," in *Giotto e il suo tempo, cit.*, Rome 1971.

F. Valcanover, "Le cause del rapido deterioramento degli affreschi della cappella Scrovegni negli ultimi venti anni," in *Giotto e il suo tempo, cit.*, Rome 1971.

C. Bellinati, "Tipologia e arte nei medaglioni della cappella di Giotto all'Arena," in *Giotto e la sua provincia*, no. 5, 1972.

C. Bellinati, "La Cappella di Giotto e le miniature dell'Antifonario 'giottesco' della cattedrale (1306)," in *Da Giotto a Mantegna*, exhibition catalogue, Padua 1974, pp. 23-30.

F. Flores D'Arcais, "Il miniatore degli Antifonari della Cattedrale di Padova: datazioni e attribuzioni," in *Bollettino del Museo Civico di Padova*, LXXVI, 1974, pp. 25-59.

D. Giunta, "Appunti sull'iconografia delle storie della Vergine nella cappella degli Scrovegni," in *Rivista dell'Istituto Nazionale d'Archeologia e Storia dell'Arte*, 1974-5.

C. Bellinati, "La cappella degli Scrovegni," in *Padova, Basiliche e Chiese*, Vicenza 1975.

W. Wolters, *La scultura veneziana gotica 1300-1460*, Venice 1976.

C. Gilbert, "The Fresco by Giotto in Milan," in *Arte Lombarda*, nos. 47-48, 1977, pp. 31-37.

L. Tintori, "Il bianco di piombo nelle pitture murali di San Francesco ad Assisi," in *Studies in Mediaeval and Renaissance Painting in Honor of M. Meiss*, New York 1977.

G. Urbani, "Studi sullo stato di conservazione della cappella degli Scrovegni di Padova," in *Bollettino d'Arte*, special series, no. 63, 1978, pp. 147 *et seq.*

M. Prosdocimi, "Classicismo in Giotto: un ricordo dei cavalli di San Marco e una citazione della Colonna Traiana," in *Bollettino del Museo Civico di Padova*, no. 68, 1979, pp. 9-14.

R.H. Rough, "Enrico Scrovegni, the 'Cavalieri Gaudenti' and the Arena Chapel in Padua," in *The Art Bulletin*, LXII, 1979.

M. Imdal, *Giotto Arenafresken: Ikonographie, Ikonologie, Ikonik*, Munich 1980.

L. Bellosi, *Giotto*, Florence 1982.

S. Osano, "Il naturalismo di Giotto e un metodo di lavoro nella sua bottega all'Arena," in *Bollettino del Museo Civico di Padova*, no. 71, 1982, pp. 25-70.

A.H. Thomas, "Dokument franziskanischer Identität: zu Datierung und Quelle der Allegorien Giottos in der Vierung der Unterkirche von San Francesco in Assisi," in *Le Congrès International de Philosophie médiévale*, Louvain-La Neuve 1982.

C. Semenzato, *La Cappella degli Scrovegni*, Padua 1983.

A.M. Spiazzi, "Giotto a Padova. I restauri della Cappella degli Scrovegni nei secoli XIX e XX," in "Giotto a Padova," in *Bollettino d'Arte*, special series, no. 2, 1983.

Var. Authors, "Giotto a Padova," in *Bollettino d'Arte, cit.*, 1983.

C. Volpe, "Il lungo percorso del 'dipingere dolcissimo e tanto unito,'" in *Storia dell'Arte Italiana*, vol. I, t. II, Turin 1983.

J. Riess, "Justice and Common Good in Giotto's Arena Chapel Frescoes," in *Arte Cristiana*, no. 701, 1984, pp. 69-80.

H.M. Thomas, "Giotto corretto: le bandiere delle schiere angeliche nella cappella degli Scrovegni," in *Bollettino del Museo Civico di Padova*, LXXIII, 1984, pp. 43-58.

L. Bellosi, *La pecora di Giotto*, Turin 1985.

G. Bonsanti, *Giotto*, Padua 1985.

C. Bellinati, "Dalla cappella di Giotto all'Arena," in *Nove secoli di campane. Simbolo arte cultura storia nella vita della gente*, exhibition catalogue, ed. by G. Cenghiaro, P.G. Nonis, Monselice 1986, pp. 67-77, 282, 292.

F. Flores d'Arcais, "Pittura del Duecento e del Trecento a Padova e nel territorio," in *La pittura in Italia. Le origini*, Milan 1986.

A. Ladis, "The Legend of Giotto's Wit and the Arena Chapel," in *The Art Bulletin*, 1986, pp. 581-96.

M.D. Edwards, "The Holly and the Ivy," in *Bollettino del Museo Civico di Padova*, LXXVI, 1987 (1989), pp. 113-26.

H.M. Thomas, "La missione di Gabriele nell'affresco di Giotto alla cappella degli Scrovegni," in *Bollettino del Museo Civico di Padova*, LXXVI, 1987 (1989), pp. 99-112.

E. Bordignon Favero, *Carte Foscari sull'Arena di Padova. La Casa Grande e la cappella degli Scrovegni*, Venice 1988.

S. Bandiera Bistoletti, *Giotto*, Florence 1989.

C. Bellinati, "Iconografia, iconologia e iconica nell'arte nuova di Giotto alla Cappella Scrovegni dell'Arena di Padova," in *Padova e il suo territorio*, IV, 21, 1989.

V. Dal Piaz, "Note per una banca dati della cappella degli Scrovegni," in *Scienza e beni culturali. Atti del Convegno*, Padua 1989.

E. Lunghi, "Giotto," in *La pittura nel Trecento, ad vocem*, vol. II, Milan 1992, pp. 524-25.

A.M. Spiazzi, "Padova," in *La pittura nel Veneto. Il Trecento*, vol. I, Milan 1992, pp. 88-177.

Photograph Credits
Sergio Anelli, Milan

Printed for Electa
by Fantonigrafica - Elemond
Editori Associati